How Animals Live and Grow

Henry Swan

ROSEN
COMMON CORE
READERS

Rosen Classroom™

New York

I0807029

Published in 2013 by The Rosen Publishing Group, Inc.
29 East 21st Street, New York, NY 10010

Copyright © 2013 by The Rosen Publishing Group, Inc.

All rights reserved. No part of this book may be reproduced in any form without permission in writing from the publisher, except by a reviewer.

Book Design: Michael Harmon

Photo Credits: Cover Cheryl E. Davis/Shutterstock.com; p. 4 Angela Waye/Shutterstock.com; p. 5 © iStockphoto.com/alxhar; p. 6 Brenda Carson/Shutterstock.com; p. 7 Anneka/Shutterstock.com; p. 8 Vishnevskiy Vasily/Shutterstock.com; p. 9 Rob McKay/Shutterstock.com; p. 10 Heiko Kiera/Shutterstock.com; p. 11 © iStockphoto.com/Pgiam; p. 12 (water alligator) Delmas Lehman/Shutterstock.com; p. 12 (land alligator) jeff gynane/Shutterstock.com; p. 13 Paul Zahl/Contributor/National Geographic/Getty Images; p. 14 Vitaly Raduntsev/Shutterstock.com; p. 15 DmZ/ Shutterstock.com; p. 16 Guy J. Sagi/Shutterstock.com; p. 17 Kjersti Joergensen/Shutterstock.com; p. 18 Betty Shelton/Shutterstock.com; p. 19 reidBETH/Shutterstock.com; p. 20 Tony Campbell/Shutterstock.com; p. 21 Monkey Business Images/Shutterstock.com; p. 22 (baby alligator) Larsek/Shutterstock.com.

ISBN: 978-1-4488-8764-4
6-pack ISBN: 978-1-4488-8765-1

Manufactured in the United States of America

CPSIA Compliance Information: Batch #WS12RC: For further information contact Rosen Publishing, New York, New York at 1-800-237-9932.

Word Count: 213

Contents

Animals live and grow in many ways!

Animals change as they grow.
This is called a life cycle.

A bird starts life as an egg.
The mother or father sits on the egg
to keep it warm and safe.

The baby bird uses its beak
to come out of the egg.

The baby bird stays in its nest
because it can't fly yet.

The baby bird learns to fly
and leaves the nest.
Now it's an adult.

Alligators come from eggs, too!

Baby alligators come out of the eggs. They live in groups called pods.

When alligators get bigger,
they are adults.
They can live in water and on land.

Goldfish also come from eggs.

A baby goldfish is called a fry.
It starts to swim and find food.

Goldfish need room to live and grow. After one year, they're adults.

A deer has its own life cycle, too.
A baby deer is called a fawn.

A mother deer goes to find food.
The fawn stays and hides.

Fawns have brown fur and white spots. The spots help them hide and stay safe.

Fawns eat grasses and other plants.
They become big deer!

Bucks are male deer.
Does are female deer.

It's fun to watch animals live and grow!

Are you growing, too?

Animal Life Cycles

bird	 egg	→  baby	→  adult
alligator	 egg	→  baby	→  adult
goldfish	 egg	→  fry	→  adult
deer	 fawn	→  deer	

Words to Know

beak

buck

doe

fry

pod

spots

Index